KU-474-914

PREDICTIONS

Crime and Punishment

STEPHEN TUMIM

PHŒNIX

A PHOENIX PAPERBACK

First published in Great Britain in 1997 by
Phoenix, a division of the Orion Publishing Group Ltd
Orion House
5 Upper Saint Martin's Lane
London, WC2H 9EA

A CIP catalogue record for this book is available
from the British Library.

ISBN 0 297 81937 2

Typeset by SetSystems Ltd, Saffron Walden
Set in 9/13.5 Stone Serif
Printed in Great Britain by
Clays Ltd, St Ives plc

Contents

Preface   vii

Introduction   1

1 The Pre-Release Course   6

2 Prison Management   13

3 Health in Prisons   26

4 Education and the Arts   34

5 The Way Ahead   40

Further Reading   53

Preface

The idea of putting together a paper, much of the content of which is taken from lectures and essays prepared over recent years, comes from the John Stuart Mill Institute, who first proposed it. The Institute is recently founded and its principal aim is 'to advance the education of the general public in social, economic and international affairs, in particular as they relate to the rights of the individual, the environment and communities'.

The paper has grown and is now broad enough, I hope, to justify publication in this series.

Introduction

In 1778, the penal reformer, John Howard, visited Rome. At San Michele, then a prison for young men, he found an inscription on the wall:

> Parum est
> Coercere improbos
> Poena
> Nisi probos efficias
> Disciplina

('It is of little use to restrain the bad by Punishment, unless you render them good by Training'.) In his book *Prisons and Lazarettos*, Howard wrote: 'This is an admirable sentence in which the grand purpose of all civil policy relative to criminals is expressed.' I am a follower of Howard.

Politicians, journalists, academics and sociologists spend a lot of time telling us what should be done to reduce crime. They are not as concise as the writer on the Roman wall. Let us start by looking at who criminals are. At Bullingdon prison in Oxfordshire there was a performance in the autumn of 1996, given mainly by prisoners, of *West Side Story*. The cast wrote their autobiographies in the programme:

I was born and grew up in London, south side. My parents came to this land from the Caribbean in the sixties and done their best for me. I have been in and out of cages since my teens and have never done drama before, though surviving in the cages is a drama in itself. I took part in this drama to escape mentally the cage I am in right now, and it's been one of the most rewarding things I've ever done in my life. We need more – it has brought things out in me that I didn't know I had.

I am a traveller, better known as a gypsy. Due to my background of travelling round the country I haven't had much education, which is part of the reason I got into trouble. I am usually an introverted person, but since I have been doing *West Side Story*, it has really brought me out of my shell. I finally feel I can do something productive. And I realize I have potential to do other things. When we first started we were all apprehensive, now I have noticed that we are all interacting with one another more easily.

I am twenty-two and come from Surrey. I am halfway through a seven-year sentence. This is the first time that I have been inside. Before my conviction I was a university student and I am now continuing my degree from within prison. I am also studying computer programming. *West Side Story* is a highly welcome diversion from normal prison life, and I understand that being a Thespian is perfectly OK, providing it is between consenting adults.

There are indeed many other types of criminal in prison: the mad, the very bad, the dangerous, the remands whose guilt is uncertain, women, the very old and the very young. But the majority, known to anyone who walks about the prisons, are inadequates, who have not, in modern parlance, got their acts together.

Before they are sent to prison they have very often committed crime, so let us look at crime before returning to its occasional sequel, punishment. Education and health are key problems for the end of the twentieth century, but the problem many people, particularly the old, find most disturbing is crime. And why is that? Statistics mislead more here than they do with most subjects, and we do not frankly know, save for our personal experience in the street, if crime against the person and property is going up or down. Whatever the figures, it affects all ages and classes, upsets and ruins lives.

A society suffers more from crime when people are poor than when almost everyone is well off. Whatever the politicians publicly pronounce, there is an obvious relationship between poverty and crime. You have only to look at the dock of a Crown Court to see who is there. Cardinal Manning put it with eloquence in the last century: 'They who live among statistics, and have seldom, if ever, lived among the poor, little know how poverty brings temptation, and temptation both vice and crime . . . It would be an affectation of scepticism to say this close relation is not by way of cause and effect.'

So one way of reducing crime is to achieve a prosperous society. But that is a long-term answer. Around our sad urban housing estates, how can you reduce the levels of crime here and now, how can you achieve a situation where citizens, including the old, can move about safely at night? The *Daily Express* (in 1996) argued that harsh conditions would help: 'The very existence of prison makes

3

many hesitate before embarking on crime and confronts the law-abiding with the knowledge that – if only for a little while – bullies, thieves and vandals are on the receiving end of nasty experience.' It may be that the prospective white-collar criminal is put off fraud from time to time by the fear of a disagreeable prison. But, although he may fear prison, I wonder if he really distinguishes, before indulging in his wrongdoing, between the toughest of prisons, such as Wandsworth, and an open prison, like Ford, as a temporary home.

I believe that the judges and the courts, governors and their prisons, have a very modest and occasional influence on the commission of crime, however firmly they discharge their duties. What puts off the burglar, the vandal, the robber, is the near certainty of capture. The police are by far the most important part of a criminal justice system, and the system, I suspect, works well where the police are known to be likely to catch the criminals. But the function of the police is by no means limited to the catching of criminals. Direct prevention of crime by encouraging citizens to take sensible steps to protect their houses and cars combines with less direct but even more valuable prevention by community policing, by encouraging other groups in the community to reveal crime, and by flooding with officers, for a necessary period, a community which is suffering from many incidents of crime.

Crime statistics, as I have said, are notoriously unreliable. Where there is difficulty, as there often is now, in getting insurance for property, the victim of theft is far less likely to report it. Police are more likely to record the vandalized purse as 'lost' rather than 'stolen'. There are many occasions when it suits the arrested criminal in the police station to agree to the court taking into consideration a list of offences of which he has never heard so as to be seen to be co-operating.

Chapter 1
The Pre-Release Course

The role of prisons turns on basic questions and answers about human nature, attitudes to and beliefs about people. Do we deter wrongdoers from more crime by treating them as a separate criminal class whose members should be excluded as fully as possible from the law-abiding community? Does punishment work in the sense that, if we punish wrongdoers fiercely enough, they will be less likely to commit further crime when they are discharged? Or does punishment work in that, if tough enough, it satisfies the rest of us and helps to exclude them from us for a while? Should prison be limited to holding those who are a danger to others because of the nature of their offences?

Would crime be reduced if we ceased to lock people up in prison, except in very exceptional circumstances, where it would be clearly dangerous to the public to let them loose? Or should we have an approach to the reduction of crime based largely on reconciliation, on closing the gap, and respecting above all the capacity of the individual to change?

It may be, as David Faulkner argues in his masterly analysis *Darkness and Light* (a 1996 report for the Howard League – named after that great eighteenth-century reformer, John Howard), that crime cannot be solely countered by any action with or against offenders. 'The origins of criminality', he writes, are often to be found in early childhood. A serious programme to reduce it should focus on support for parents and children in difficulty, and opportunities for young people entering upon adult life. It should also recognize the too often neglected problems of mental disorder among children in adolescence. Programmes to prevent crime by physical means, including video cameras and close-circuit television, can be of value, but their effects will be limited and local unless action is also taken to change the motivation of offenders and those at risk of offending.

The criminal justice process, he is saying, cannot be the principal means of preventing or reducing crime.

I do not believe there can be any certainty about the extent to which punishment will ever seriously reduce crime. Prison can be used to replace the failed school, or as a substitute, however inadequate, for the family. It keeps the serious criminal out of the way for a time, but the key question remains: where does the criminal go, what does he do, when he comes back into the community?

Punishment is inflicted by the court, which has to take into account issues of public protection, deterrence, denunciation, compensation and rehabilitation, and, above all, what is just in the circumstances. Punishment in Britain may consist of the confiscation of money, the compulsion of community service or the deprivation of liberty. The deprivation is, as Alexander Paterson, the greatest leader of the Prison Service of the mid-twentieth century, famously, but rather obscurely, told us, 'as punishment', not 'for punishment'. The rate of imprisonment is higher in this country than almost anywhere else in Western Europe and there may be a sizeable number of prisoners who could sensibly be dealt with in the community.

But the media and many of their readers and viewers regard punishment as coming not so much from the court as from those who are carrying out the sentence of the court. In particular they expect punishment to be inflicted by the Prison Service through making prison life harsher. There are two main reasons for this quest. One of them is the satisfaction commonly derived by the godly from the sufferings of the ungodly. The other is the belief that if a man has a bad enough time during his sentence he will be unlikely to commit further crime – though that is not a belief founded on historical experience. Both reasons raise questions about the relationship of punishment to crime, and, for me at any rate, they are most aptly approached by looking at the prison system.

What are prisons for? Ever since the modern concept of imprisonment was established by Jeremy Bentham, our first major utilitarian philosopher, around the end of the eighteenth century, prison has been the prime instrument used by the criminal justice system to attempt to reduce the rate of crime. The American Declaration of Independence in 1776, a principal event in the history of British prisons, had ended transportation to America, while South Africa and Australia were not yet used for housing British convicts. Punishment in Britain became harsher, and many more offences attracted the death penalty, yet the crime rate went up and up. Punishment by long-term deprivation of liberty, deliberately aimed at improving the behaviour of prisoners and reducing the rate of crime, came in soon after the new century. Now we have far more than a hundred prisons, some being used for women, others for the young, the dangerous or those needing to learn the skills of resettlement in the community.

If we are to rely on prisons to reduce the crime rate, whom do we decide to lock up? The majority of prisoners are male and well under thirty. They are young men who have failed at school or have been failed by school. They have weak (if any) family links. Their offences are mainly concerned with drink, drugs and motor cars, and stealing money to acquire more. They come from impoverished city areas. If they are violent, it is not planned, but part of their social inadequacy. Their time in prison is usually somewhere around a year and they will then return to the community from which they came. They have about a half a century before them as citizens of our country.

How do we fulfil the purpose of prison to reduce the crime rate, as far as this majority is concerned? We want to make our cities safer, reduce the burglaries and ensure there are fewer victims. If we warehouse them and simply ensure they live in custody in harsh and insanitary conditions, are we going to deter this majority from crime when their year or whatever is up? Or would such treatment – while not unreasonably pleasing to some law-abiding citizens – cause this majority of prisoners irrevocably to lose self-respect and drive them into lives of alternating crime and punishment? Idleness corrupts.

There can surely be only one answer to how we are to reduce the crime rate with this majority of prisoners. Unless we are to lock them up for their lives, the process must be to treat prison as an active pre-release course, so that the majority of the majority leave prison with self-respect and the capacity and intention to live as proper citizens.

This majority group urgently requires the formal education that will enable them to manage in the community. Many of them are essentially competent young men who have yet to get their acts together and learn the dangers of unlawful drugs. There are a surprising number of young near-illiterates in prison, who, although not stupid, need support in reading, writing and arithmetic. The ratio of illiterates to non-illiterates among prisoners is around three times higher than would be found in their home communities. We need to re-examine the prison education curriculum, too often based on what teachers like to teach or on unrealistic ideas of what is needed. They will be returning to a community where unskilled work will be increasingly hard to find.

The majority need the moral education they have not had in the family. They need to learn to face their offending behaviour, as our prevailing jargon calls it. In ordinary English they need to learn the difference between right and wrong and to learn how to behave. They need to learn how to conduct themselves at job interviews, and the practice of work. They need to learn that a degree in street wisdom is insufficient to enable them to lead law-abiding and useful lives. They need to learn to respect potential victims and to lead law-abiding lives while out of employment.

Where possible, they should be helped to build family links. We should be establishing clusters of prisons, each cluster within one management system, so that the prisoner can be kept in his home area, yet transferred between prisons of differing regimes as he progresses and where he can be provided with the necessary security and training. There is a far greater chance of imprisonment reducing the crime rate if the prisoner happens to have a law-abiding and supportive family. Inevitably there are a number of prisoners, among the majority and otherwise, who have no potential family links or only undesirable ones. There are not methods of improvement which can be applied successfully to every prisoner.

For most prisoners, including the large group I have styled the majority, custody is a comparatively short interruption, sometimes repeated, in a life of liberty. Prison regimes for short-term prisoners must be about returning to liberty. The content of the regime programmes should be drawn from the community itself. A local prison, a prison in a cluster, is part of the community. What are the conditions of education, training and employment which exist for young people in the area who are not in trouble with the law? What facilities does the community make available to them? Whatever local arrangements, they should be extended for use within the prison system, so that the prisoner on release does not enter a wholly alien world in relation to training or work. Programmes within the prison should correspond with those available in the community. On discharge, a prisoner should be able to complete a training course or work experience outside. Local employers should be asked to advise or even assist with an industrial prison by investing in work space in the prison. Preparation for release must be genuine and realistic, if prisoners are going to get work after discharge in the community. Useful prisons only come about with community support. Prisons are not separate institutions although they separate inmates from the rest of us. They are there to reduce the crime rate largely by reintegrating the majority of prisoners into normal life.

Educating and training the majority of prisoners, running a prison as a pre-release course, requires patience and constant devotion to duty by the Service, the education officers, chaplains and probation officers and all who work in prisons. The job of replacing the failed schools, the broken families, within what is often a matter of months rather than years, is exceedingly demanding. It will not succeed every time. It should reduce crime. It will not end it.

Chapter 2
Prison Management

Over my eight years as HM Chief Inspector of Prisons (1987–95), it became clear to me that those who are responsible for framing penal policy need to see a great deal of prison life, to listen to governors, staff and prisoners. The cartoon picture of prisoners, stout persons sending out officers for lobsters and grouse, the young enjoying a holiday-camp existence, are entirely misleading; but, as in every institution, very occasional examples of abuse can always be found by those who want them for propaganda.

The Chief Inspector can do a lot to demonstrate the truth. The Inspectorate of Prisons was established by statute in 1982. The Chief Inspector is appointed by Royal Warrant. He has to inspect or arrange for inspections of prisons, and to report to the Home Secretary on what he finds: in particular on the treatment of prisoners and conditions in prisons. He conducts enquiries when so directed. He produces reviews on prison subjects which he believes may be relevant for Ministers. He reports annually to Parliament. In addition to his statutory duties he fulfils a heavy programme of public communication. He needs to explain his reports and proposals in broadcasts, in newspapers and in conference speeches. He has a role to play in publicizing the Prison Service and in bringing together as best he can various branches of the criminal justice system. But primarily he has to inspect the prisons.

The Chief Inspector is provided with a staff of about twenty. They include three former very senior prison governors and some less senior former members of the Prison Service and some Home Office Principals. Research, medical, building and other consultants are called in as they are needed. While they work in the Inspectorate they share the Chief Inspector's independence, although most of them later return to the Prison Service or the Home Office. Independence is at the heart of the Inspectorate's structure. The Chief Inspector is a layman in relation to the people he inspects, staff and inmates alike. He has right of access to all prisons. His reports are published.

An independent lay Inspectorate is an exceedingly unusual creature. Most Chief Inspectors in the criminal justice field and elsewhere, although they have laymen on their staff, are themselves of the profession being inspected. The Chief Inspector of Constabulary is by background a policeman. The Chief Inspectors of Social Services and of Probation have been life members of the profession they inspect. This will bring the advantages of both knowledge and experience of the issues. But if a principal task of an inspector is to ask very basic questions and to press for answers, then the advantage may lie with a layman. He is not inspecting former colleagues. The Service knows that it cannot respond to criticism with the equivalent of 'Well, we have always done it this way,' and expect this to be accepted. A lay chief inspector needs to have highly professional and skilled advisers. He must bear in mind that he is Her Majesty's Chief Inspector, with a duty to advise Ministers. He does not head a pressure group. He is an adviser, not part of any line management. His very independence must remind him of the need to be exceedingly responsible. The Citizen's Charter sets it all out very clearly: the Inspectorate 'has right of access to all prisons, and to the Home Secretary, to whom it reports its conclusions and recommendations. Its reports are public and available to Parliament. The Government will ensure that the Prisons Inspectorate remains strong and independent in the future.' The appointment of my successor, General Sir David Ramsbotham, in 1995, honoured that commitment.

There are a number of guides offering help not only to the prison staff, but to management and policymakers at national and local levels. First, there is the Prison Service's short and admirable 'Statement of Purpose', which is hung prominently in every prison: 'Her Majesty's Prison Service serves the public by keeping in custody those committed by the Court. Our duty is to look after them with humanity and help them lead law-abiding and useful lives in custody and after release.' I know no other institution with a more memorable and sharp self-direction. Prisons, at any rate for the majority of prisoners, should be run as pre-release centres. From the moment the convicted criminal goes to prison he should be actively helped to lead a law-abiding and useful life. The 'Statement of Purpose' is a sound text for an inspector to apply. The bad prison is one where the prisoner is in his cell and on his bed at midday. The good prison is one where the tests are not of niceness and nastiness, those sentimental qualities, but of how active the prisoner is during the day, in law-abiding and useful occupation. The 'Statement' expresses very clearly the necessary case against institutionalizing the prisoner.

Second, there is the Woolf Report. After the disturbances

around Easter 1990 at Strangeways and other prisons, Lord Justice Woolf investigated the events themselves with the help of counsel, and thereafter led an examination (in which I joined Lord Justice Woolf) into the problems of the prisons and the Prison Service. The result was a monumental report which both analysed the disturbances themselves and proposed solutions for the grievances of prisoner and staff which he found to be at the centre of the troubles. It remains a report of the greatest importance.

While the Woolf Report was in preparation, in late 1990, the Inspectorate produced a thematic review, at the request of the Prisons' Minister, on *Suicide and Self-Harm in Prisons*. The report included an examination of precautions and attitudes and a comparison between health-care provision in prison and in the National Health Service. It was designed in particular to look at the anxieties, often leading to self-harm, felt by the young entering prison on remand or conviction for the first time. It made more than 100 recommendations, of which the great majority were concerned with attitudes and modest material changes capable of being put into effect at little cost.

In the autumn of 1991 were published the most important guidelines of all, namely the Government White Paper, *Custody, Care and Justice: The Way Ahead for the Prison Service in England and Wales* (for the purposes of convenience, in this paper England includes Wales). This was the first occasion on which a British government has ever produced a full statement of long-term plans for the prisons. It was specifically stated to be a design for the rest of the century and beyond. The White Paper is based on both the reports referred to above.

Prison management has to hold the balance between security, humanity and helping prisoners to lead law-abiding lives. There is no average prison and no average prisoner. The dangerous prisoner, perhaps a terrorist or serial murderer, requires above all a secure containment, so that he cannot escape and cause harm. All prisoners must be protected against violence from other prisoners and need to be looked after humanely. Some prisoners, the elderly dishonest for example, need a far lower and less expensive form of security. Others, the less violent young, need help in growing into maturity.

It must be remembered that the dangerous prisoners are a very small percentage of the whole and that non-violent young and uneducated males constitute a majority of those held in custody. The dangerous amount to perhaps 2 or 3 per cent of the total, but it is they who make it necessary for us to pay for heavy security. The cameras and dogs, the high and strengthened walls, the electric equipment, all need, and do not always get, constant checking. Prisoners often escape not through a weakness in the hardware, but through a failure in its use. Constant and irregular searching of the cells of dangerous men, counting them as they are moved around the prison, continual checking of checks themselves, require high morale among staff, encouragement and supervision.

The categorization of prisoners, following the escape of the spy George Blake from Wormwood Scrubs in 1966 and the ensuing Mountbatten Report, is based on the need for security rather than control, so that every possible step is taken to see that the dangerous do not escape from the prison. Control is more an internal matter, so that staff may ensure that gangs of criminals are broken up and that internal prison life remains under the eyes of staff. The immediate interest of the community is more in security than in control, so that the dangerous at any rate remain behind the walls and do not escape. But there are problems in ignoring the needs for control in categorizing prisoners. At Wymott in 1993, the prisoners took control from the staff, broke up the prison and terrified the weaker inmates, although there was no serious attempt at escape. The gangs needed firm control, although they did not form much of a security risk in the Mountbatten sense, and were therefore put in Category C. We need to ensure proper control, as well as to maintain the necessary security, particularly among prisoners who come from the drug culture of young urban Britain.

Those on remand, the unconvicted, form in all countries a prison problem of their own. The philosophical difficulties in getting activity out of the idle, who are deemed not guilty until they are convicted, are evidenced at the Wolds, where the excellent facilities were, when I inspected, insufficiently used by prisoners, who preferred to loiter. Probably a secure bail hostel is a better model than a prison for a remand centre. There is no reason why a hostel, well run, should not have rules which encourage an active life. Prisoners should also be brought more speedily to trial. I frequently met remand prisoners who had been held for over a year. The remand population are a temperamental group, nervous about their situation and – not surprisingly – about loss of rights.

Women prisoners raise quite different problems. The women's prison population is at record levels and rising.

In October 1996, their numbers stood at more than 2,300, around 15 per cent more than the year before, and about 50 per cent more than in 1993. Despite the rising population, relatively few women are serving sentences for very serious offences. The 1995 figures show that as in previous years a great many of them are remand prisoners or are serving sentences for fine default or property offences, rather than violent or sexual offences. It is desirable that prisons should be grouped in areas, so that most prisoners can be held within reach of their families, and so that staff and their families can settle down without too much prospect of being moved. But it is impractical to provide suitable prisons for women in each area and to cover the various desirable regimes. The most dangerous tend to be placed in Durham, often hundreds of miles from their children. Holloway, in London, holds women with greatly varying needs, and often subjects them to wholly unsuitable treatment.

Young offenders present the most difficult problem. The catchment areas are often too large, so that boys from Cornwall or Liverpool are held at Feltham, near Slough, remote from their communities. The institutions are often too big. At Feltham nearly 800 teenagers are held. Our cultural attitude to the young becomes more relevant. We are fully conscious that they are offenders but remain far less conscious that they are young. Very few staff are trained to deal specifically with teenagers: many of them have spent the bulk of their careers with adults.

The Young Offenders Institutions (YOI), where those under twenty-one are held, are not sufficiently distinguished, save by name, from the ordinary prison. The institutions nevertheless vary greatly in quality. In all of them there is some admirable work by staff. But the job of helping the criminal teenager lead a law-abiding and useful life after release is an exceedingly demanding one. In far too many establishments the young are largely ware-housed, and discharged without the skills or the self-respect which are likely to protect society from further villainy. The recidivism rate for the young remains in the area of 80 per cent reconvicted within two years of dis-charge. Bullies must be checked. If we bully the bullies in the course of training them, they become better-trained, more efficient bullies. The outstanding model YOI at pres-ent is Lancaster Farms in Lancashire (see Chapter 5). It shows what can be achieved.

The problem with young offenders is that in their treat-ment the accent falls on the second word and not on the first. To an inspector on a visit it seems eccentric that these children, often young for their ages, are under the control of prison staff rather than teachers and those trained to look after the very young. As David Faulkner pointed out, develop-ments, including the demonizing of children, perhaps at its peak in the Bulger case, and the society's growing urge to exclude young offenders, thereby deliberately widening the gap between wrongdoers and the community, have rein-forced the 'justice' approach, by which children are expected to take responsibility for their actions, and have added a more punitive element to it. It is true that differing views of human nature lie at the heart of our divergent views on custody, but the media and the state, in adopting this approach, seem to be adopting a somewhat medieval attitude.

Some young offenders are now to go to boot camps and

into military glasshouses. My successor as Chief Inspector has made his comments:

> For the life of me, I can see little point in forming young civilian offenders up in threes and marching them around. In the army there is a purpose – to train people to obey orders in battle. What I would favour is a challenging regime including work, education, the opportunity to build self-esteem and hopefully bring out the best qualities in young offenders. They should end the day exhausted but proud of what they have achieved. It would be similar to the schemes run by the Outward Bound Trust – though certainly no safaris at taxpayers' expense.

Most prisoners need to learn the practice of work, and this is not limited to what I have termed the majority. We should introduce the industrial prison. The industrial prison is one where work comes first. Education and sport are available only at the end of a working day. An outside company employs the prisoners to make goods. The company pays the industrial wage and provides materials and machinery. The Prison Service, which supervises the work, takes a cut, and the prisoners are paid wages according to how hard and skilfully they work. The prisoners pay tax and insurance on their earnings. Their net earnings are divided, after discussion with prison officials, between their families and their own savings. Instead of 'private cash' in small amounts being paid for prisoners by their families, the money goes the other way. Relations are improved between prisoner and family. Social Security for the family may be reduced. The prisoner leaves prison with substantial savings, working skills and the habit of work.

All this to some extent happens in Germany and in other European countries. It operates to the advantage of everybody, although more so in a period of fairly full employment and with the agreement of the unions.

In England the industrial prison has been tested out at Coldingley, where it has failed – probably because the prisoners are restricted to pocket money. They are paid by the state a few pounds a week. They are not allowed to earn anything approaching full wages, and there are very few prisoners in England earning more than £10 weekly. Prisoners, unfortunately, will not work hard eight hours a day in order to repay their moral debt to society. If you walk into a workshop in any English prison, heads turn: the mood is one of apathy. If you go into a German prison where men are employed at acceptable wages – lower in fact than a full industrial wage – you will find the atmosphere of an efficient factory, where contract terms have to be met. If an industrial prison is to work, the prisoners must be paid as workers or given some other compensation, such as substantial shortening of sentence.

Some people spend most of their lives in prison. Is it possible to develop a quality of life, a useful life, in such an environment? Long-term prisons can be productive places, where the ability to work, to earn, to give something to society, can be valued. Such prisons are useful to the rest of us. The approach which I find myself adopting after some eight years' independent inspection is that education for the majority and properly paid – much of it skilled – work are the keys to reducing the crime rate. What are the counter-arguments put forward on prisons in the media debate on law and order?

The most often repeated argument has the virtue of brevity. 'Prison works,' it is said. This means, I think, that while a man is held in prison he cannot commit a crime outside. But, unless all prisoners are to be held for their natural lives, the phrase seems empty, if the aim of custody is to reduce the crime rate. 'Prison works' could have another meaning, that some prisons work effectively, so that prisoners are discharged from them ready to lead law-abiding lives. We have in England a number of excellent institutions. My reports referred to some local and training prisons, some YOI and some resettlement prisons where prison is working very well. Indeed, at the resettlement prisons, the English penal system is breaking fresh ground. These prisons, of which Blantyre House in Kent was the first, take serious criminals with appalling records and long sentences and prepare them towards the end of their sentences for working and living in the community. Many prisoners from there go out daily to work and earn full outside wages. The sanction is that if they take drugs or misbehave they are liable to be sent to a harsher prison. It seems to work. So if the phrase 'Prison works' is to be construed as 'Some prisons can work' my reports would strongly support it.

But the slogan 'Some prisons can work' may have less public support than one might wish. Prisons hold the prisoners and it is sufficient that while inside they cannot harm innocent people; thereafter they may be deterred by the experience from the possibility of return. There are others, including many of the expert criminologists of the last thirty years, who would say that no prison works, that criminals should be treated outside. This group and the

'Prison works' group have much in common. Neither believes that anything useful can be done in prison.

Another phrase reverberates through media discussion. 'We must not spend more on training and helping the criminal than we do on the non-criminal.' This appears inconsistent with the aim of imprisonment, if it is to reduce the crime rate. It may be necessary to educate or re-educate the prisoner, particularly if he comes from the majority group. It seems unlikely that a man will commit a crime in order to take advantage of prison education, whether it is academic, social or moral. But it is important to remember that, if it is to be effective, the help given to prisoners must be direct and immediate. They must be kept busy and not left lolling around most of the day in their cells. Society needs here as elsewhere – in that great cant phrase of the age – to achieve value for money.

What of the cost of improvement? We already have a set of teachers in every prison. We already have a prison staff which is as responsible a set of individuals as any staff elsewhere. The provision of education and work in order to reduce the rate of crime does not require massive new resources. Indeed the adoption of the industrial prison should, as it does in Germany, actually produce a financial profit for the prison.

A traditional definition of punishment is the infliction of a penalty in retribution for an offence, a penalty imposed to ensure the application or enforcement of the law. Retribution and deterrence should certainly be taken into account in schemes designed to reduce crime. A more recent approach, and perhaps a more effective one, empha-sizes the need to repair relationships damaged by crime, an approach now called 'relational justice', or, in New Zealand in particular, 'restorative justice'. The Woolf Report and the White Paper acknowledge in our penal system the lack of satisfactory relations between prisoner and prisoner, prisoner and prison officer, prison officer and governor, and governor and headquarters, and between the various agencies of the criminal justice system. These reports were in large part an attempt to ensure that justice was not seen to have stopped at the prison gates, and that grievances would be fully and honestly examined. 'Relational justice', David Faulkner has written, 'is not offered as a paradigm or a comprehensive test of all public policy, but relational values can provide an important and often new perspective, an interconnected set of ideas which can help to illuminate issues, indicate the directions in which future policies might lead, and provide a new dynamic for reform.'

That perspective can best be approached by adopting the advice we encounter on the London Underground: 'Mind the gap'. Where relations have broken down, where there is a void between the wrongdoer and society, there is a choice between the 'Prison works' philosophy, broadening the gap into a moat, and the philosophy which aims to educate the wrongdoer and reconcile him to society. There is no inconsistency between doing more to address the needs of victims and respecting the rights of offenders.

Chapter 3
Health in Prisons

It has been said that medical care in prisons is a dull form of general practice, or even a grotesque form. There are few problems of children or childbirth or old age. The patients are mainly healthy young men, although there is a high level of complaint about treatment or lack of treatment. There are always too many patients coming to the surgery out of boredom. It is hardly surprising that it is difficult to attract medical practitioners of high skill and enthusiasm into the Service.

In the Woolf Report of 1991 Lord Woolf and I said remarkably little about prison medical services, partly because we felt that such services were only very loosely connected with the disturbances of April 1990, and partly because the *Scrutiny Report on the Prison Medical Service* was then awaited from the Government Efficiency Unit. But we did state firmly: 'Prisoners and their families must feel confident that the medical treatment prisoners receive in prison is of comparable standard to that which they would receive in normal life from the National Health Service.' In one respect such treatment is often superior to what inmates would receive outside: access to medicine in prison is often far more prompt than in a hard-pressed community health centre. It is the quality of some of the treatment with which we must be concerned.

In 1992 there was an alteration in the arrangements for

medical service which Joe Pilling, then Director-General of the Prison Service, proclaimed as a 'celebration of change'. In my annual report for the year, I wrote:

> The replacement of a Medical Service by a Health Care Service gives a far higher prominence to preventive medicine. It greatly extends the work of the Service. The Director [of the Health Care Service] has pledged it to more consultation of patients as to how they want things done. We must now expect, and indeed hope for, useful pronouncements and advice from the new Service in such areas as food and diet and hours of meals, the state of the kitchens, time out of cell, and the need for physical and mental exercise. The continuing lack of a gym for nearly a thousand remands at Brixton (the present gym being outside the secure area) is a matter for health care comment by those working under the Director of Health Care.

If that change of attitude is to be more than a modish choice of language, we must look again at the standing of the prison doctor in relation to the Prison Service. We must note that the Health Care Service, the old Prison Medical Service, has an astonishing number of admirals as compared to sailors: more than almost anywhere in the Prison Service, it is grossly overweighted with those bearing higher rank in the Civil Service. But this, although an extravagance, is not a cause of unrest.

One of the most important tasks that I had to perform as an independent Chief Inspector of Prisons was to promote the appreciation among prison staff that they have a valuable and very difficult role to play in society; and to convey the view to the general public that prisons and those who work in them discharge heavy responsibilities on behalf of the rest of us. In other areas of public life which have similar value to the community, it is not necessary to make the point so often. Although in England we appear to be too ready to minimize the status of many groups of valuable workers – social workers and teachers come to mind – the Prison Service does seem to require particular support. If I am right that the Prison Service does not enjoy high public regard, I believe that the effects of this bear also upon those specialists who work in prisons, among whom, of course, are prison doctors and medical staff. (I use the word specialists, not in the medical sense, but of someone who works professionally in prison but not in the ordinary Prison Service.)

Among prison staff, the career route from officer to Governor may follow a number of diverse paths, but the experience gained by an individual, and the recognition of that experience, will occur within the Prison Service. By contrast, the specialist worker within the prison comes from outside, with a professional identity created elsewhere. Training and experience as a teacher, doctor or psychologist are acquired through educational and professional institutions, which are of course part of the community. Only later is that experience applied to the prison context. I believe that the source of tension between specialists and main grade staff is partly to be found in the difference between the career structures of the individuals concerned. Add to this the fact that prison staff routinely work with inmates, whereas some specialist staff come in to provide services, then depart, and it is possible to understand the often expressed view of the prison officer that 'They cannot know what it is *really* like.'

In the early 1990s efforts have been made to integrate the Prison Service into the wider community, through the development of such ideas as the community prison, prison open days, and work programmes for prisoners within the community. As we have noted, the Woolf Report states that medical treatment for inmates should be of the same standard as the ordinary population would receive on the National Health Service. The report made it clear that the standard of medical care on offer in prison establishments frequently failed to reach this level.

Prison medical services appear to remain largely uncoordinated. Some establishments still have unused hospital accommodation and under-employed staff whilst others struggle, even to ensure that all inmates are medically screened, however briefly, on reception. Advisory health programmes are virtually non-existent. We must press again for regular medical and dental check-ups for lifers and long-termers, and for blood pressure and urine testing as part of a reception screening process which also includes a confidential interview with the doctor who will be responsible for the inmates on-going health care.

Few would doubt that there is room for improvement in prison medical services. The comment in the Woolf Report reflects more detailed concerns expressed over many years within the medical profession, by outside commentators and by my own specialist inspectors. Since 1939, many reports have highlighted the problems associated with the provision of medical services in prisons – the East-

Hubert Report of 1939, the Gwynne Report of 1964, the Butler Report of 1975, the Report of the Royal College of Psychiatrists in 1979 and the 1986 Report of the Social Services Committee of the House of Commons. In 1990, the Hoffenberg Working Party aimed to bring the Prison Medical Service more under the guidance of the Royal College of Physicians, and at the same time a scrutiny of the Prison Medical Service was carried out by the Government Efficiency Unit. Finally a full report on the training and education of doctors in the Health Care Service for Prisoners prepared by the three Royal Colleges, of Physicians, General Practitioners and Psychiatrists, was published in about 1992.

One of the suggestions that have been made to improve the situation is that medical services in prisons should be provided by the NHS, bought in the same way that probation and education services are at present. It has also been suggested that prison medicine should be seen as a medical specialty, with practitioners specially trained for the role. I think that both these ideas have merit, but they do not fully address the problems posed by the practice of medicine in prisons. I would like to use both ideas as the basis for an alternative suggestion.

A large number of small, or low-security, prison establishments have had medical services provided by doctors from the NHS (normally GPs, providing a number of sessions in each week) for many years. The problem centres on large prisons, which require a full-time medical staff. The attraction of the handover of such complex and closed establishments to the already beleaguered NHS is, I believe, limited. Although many hospital trusts would like to provide the service, costs have so far been prohibitive. No one is suggesting that prison medicine can be a medical speciality in the same way as oncology, cardiology or orthopaedics, but it is specialized insofar as it requires knowledge of public health and prison administrative matters which the ordinary GP would not need. Prisoners are members of the general population in particular circumstances. The medical services required, therefore, are the services required by the general population, with the addition of particular links with psychiatric and forensic services which form part of the additional responsibility of the Head of Medical Services in a prison. The Head of Medical Services, therefore, acts primarily as a GP and in this capacity should be the first port of call for someone who is sick. This general practice role is supported by many of the recently published reports on prison medicine.

I believe that prison populations are worthy of specialist study within the GP subject areas. There is a need for systematic work to be undertaken on the sociomedical characteristics of the prison population, as well as on specifically medical questions relating to the presentation and treatment of illness in the prison environment. It would be helpful for the Prison Health Service to encourage links with the Departments of Community Medicine and Public Health in the DHSS to promote work on the social aspects of prison medicine and for the general practice aspect of medicine in prison to be recognized as an area requiring some special training by the three Royal Colleges. This training should be subject to review and accreditation by the Royal Colleges.

It is a welcome development that the three Royal Colleges

have co-operatively examined prison medical issues, and we must look to their recommendations on the most appropriate means to prepare doctors for work in the prison context. There is no doubt that doctors who work full-time in prisons require regular and mandatory access to training programmes which not only update and extend knowledge about issues pertinent to the practice of medicine in prisons, but which also bring the prison doctor into contact with medical colleagues working in other areas of medicine. There is a status issue here which needs to be addressed. Prison doctors must be able to earn professional status equivalent to their colleagues. This is not difficult for those part-time medical officers who also work in general practice. It is more difficult for the full-time medical officers.

In this way doctors (and other health care staff, such as nurses, for whom similar conditions should apply) would maintain their professional expertise. Professional well-being demands that such contacts are maintained. The closed work of the prison has in the past tended to remove specialists from this contact. The mainstream Prison Service has much to gain, not only in the improvement to specialist services that would result from suggestions that I have made here in respect of medicine; but also from the possible application of such arrangements to the work of mainstream prison staff. Above all, it would provide a sound basis for the provision of real health care for prisoners.

The system at present seems particularly defective in relation to severe mental disorder. In a recent study by Professor Gunn of the Maudsley Hospital, the incidence of such disorder among remand prisoners seems shocking: over half the remands professionally examined suffered from psychiatric disorder, including 5 per cent with psychosis. Many men with severe mental disorder were placed on busy wings where, as the report says, 'the quietly mad are ignored'.

One of society's major health problems, in and out of prison, is caused by drug abuse. In July 1994 two very experienced inspectors, a former senior governor and a consultant psychiatrist visited Styal, a women's prison in Cheshire. There inmates asserted, and staff agreed, that drugs brought in by visitors and inmates who had been on home leave were freely available in the prison. The visitors were told that almost all inmates used cannabis, a large proportion took opiates, mainly heroin, probably about half took cocaine or crack, and a lesser proportion took amphetamines and occasionally LSD. They were given to understand that more than half took benzodiazepines and that more than half of those who injected shared needles. The Inspectorate called for a full medical assessment and the Prison Service did not respond. The picture we were given was among the worst we have come across during all our inspections, although there are many other prisons with a serious and uncontrolled drug problem.

Chapter 4
Education and the Arts

Beside the need for true and efficient health care stands the need for education, in the three senses of school, moral and social education. Education is urgently needed in particular for the majority of prisoners I have described, those young men with specific problems of lack of school and family. Education is needed not only by this large group, but by most other prisoners too. Education for prisoners is as much for our benefit as for theirs, and the cuts in education effected by government from about 1995 are going to be as damaging to the rest of the community as to the prisoners. A governor cannot limit security, food or health easily, so he cuts education. This is sad and ominous, perhaps more dangerous to the future of the law-abiding public even than the prison riots of 1990 which led to the Woolf Report, the rules for useful prisons as set out in the White Paper which followed the Woolf Report and an improved professional Prison Service.

I talked recently to three young men in a London prison, all due out in a month or two, about the problems of poverty they will face when they are released. How would they earn a decent living? Where would they live? They had no answers, had had no help and sadly expected to return to prison. The reduction of the number of probation officers working in prison (part of the cuts) and of education and care will not help them lead law-abiding lives.

We ought not to forget the place of the arts in prison education. I have had a particular concern with this as a result of a connection with the Koestler Fund, which is designed to help people held in prisons, young offender institutions, youth treatment centres, secure units and special hospitals. The Koestler Awards are designed to raise the self-respect of inmates and patients by giving them a cultural objective and a valuable opportunity for beneficial self-expression. The first casualty in cuts appears always to be education and the arts.

Arthur Koestler, the writer and sage, was imprisoned in Spain in the Civil War and sentenced to death. He got out, but was imprisoned in France and, when he eventually reached England, in Pentonville prison. He came to believe that prisoners – and those held against their will in mental hospitals – needed the self-respect that comes from being stimulated to create. Their painting, craft, writing, music, anything they made that was shapely, was to be publicly exhibited. Prizes were to be given. It was to be an annual event.

The Koestler Awards scheme was introduced into our prisons and special hospitals in 1961, with the active support of the then Home Secretary, Rab Butler. It has been a clear success under the leadership of Sir Hugh Casson and David Astor. Competition judges give their services free. The Home Office has supported us with an annual grant and a prison to work from. It remains, however, essential for retaining the support of prisoners that these awards are given by an independently funded, unofficial body. This was an important part of Koestler's intuitive perception and is regarded by prison people as vital.

Prisons are noisy and overcrowded places. Prisoners are continuously under stress of one kind or another. One system of improvement is the practice of the arts: theatre, drawing and painting, writing, craft and music. All demand concentration, and the time spent is rewarded by increasing skill. Theatre may have the most value, because teamwork, words, speech, music, visual themes are all needed. The acquisition of even a modest skill gives satisfaction and self-respect.

So the first purpose of the arts in prison is to help with the main purpose of imprisonment: the reduction of future crime. Art in prison is a legitimate instrument for healing wounds. Most prisoners arrive to serve their sentences bitter and confused. From practising an art they derive a sense of order. It is interesting to see what our greatest art therapist, the late Edward Adamson, had to say. He practised for many years in a mental hospital rather than a prison. But the principles he worked out and applied would be fit for hospital or prison. He understood the importance of providing a sanctuary, a space in which the connection could be made between creativity and healing. His genius lay in his ability to create the 'enabling space'. He was a believer in what Jung called 'the art of letting things happen'.

Edward Adamson believed that the teacher should not teach but should be as passive as possible, never attempting to interpret the person's work, particularly when he or she was painting. He did not want pictures designed to please him but work which expressed quite freely the dynamics of the person's thoughts. They were tools for diagnosis by the doctors, but were also sharp and original works in their own right.

Not only does the best prison painting give the prisoner some self-respect, it helps him counter the gloom of the prison and makes him less likely to return to crime.

The effect on the artist is more interesting than the effect on the viewer. In 1996 I judged a competition at a large London prison. There were three winners. One had painted an illustration of *Wuthering Heights*, with Heathcliff as a ghost crossing a stream, followed by the heroine. 'Why a ghost?' I asked. He explained at great length, and fairly convincingly, and then poured out the story of the murder he had committed and his mental condition, the belief of a secure mental hospital that they could treat him successfully, the inexplicable transfer to a prison, the lack of further treatment. The painting and the prize he won had got him thinking more clearly.

Another winner was a young man who had made a most accurate model of a caravan from matchsticks. He told me it was his family caravan. He was a gypsy, and he had lived in it in what he thought of as his peaceful period before his first offence. He wanted, he said, to return home. The third winner was an enormous young man from Uganda. He had painted vast woods and forests in the style – slightly – of Gainsborough, and skies in the manner of Constable. 'How do you come to choose this style?' I asked. 'I am really an eighteenth-century man,' he said. (Rousseau would have been interested.) He was recovering only very slowly from a drug-induced illness.

The succession of plays, mainly musicals, performed in

the London prisons with the help of Pimlico Opera and other benefactors has been impressive. *West Side Story* has been most movingly performed at both Wandsworth and Bullingdon prisons. I liked in particular the catalogues, where the performers record their views of life. Listen to this one:

I was born in St Anne's Bay, Jamaica. My mum and dad had me at an early age, she was 16 and my dad was 18. My dad died when I was four years old. My mum came to England when she was 20 to study to be an accountant. I stayed in Jamaica with my grandparents, aunts and uncles. When I was seven my mum came back to Jamaica to get me, which made me really happy because by that time I was always getting a beating and I was thinking she didn't want me.

Coming to this country was a big shock, but I got used to it. My first day at school was a disaster. It started as a fight and when I finally got kicked out of school, it was for stabbing a teacher. I had just turned 12 years old in secondary school. After that it was children's homes then prisons. I started coming to prison because of the violence, but I soon met up with the wrong crowd and I started taking drugs and getting into more crime. That's why I am at Wandsworth now. At the moment I am trying to channel all my energy into something positive, *West Side Story*. The main reason is because everyone that I am working with are sensible and fun to work with. I am enjoying myself very much. I would like to say thanks.

'Prison art' is a misleading phrase. There is no art unique to prisoners. But if we believe prisons are intended to help prisoners lead law-abiding and useful lives, then we must recognize that our chances of success are limited without provision for the arts. In 1995 in particular government policy appeared to involve saving money and looking for votes by cutting down on education and the arts in prison. That is the way to increase crime.

Chapter 5
The Way Ahead

To describe the worst and the best of our penal institutions is one way of explaining the problem and its cure.

Most of the bad prisons were ones I saw early in my employment, and a fair specimen was Risley Remand Centre, as it was in 1988. My report of that year described the prisoners' treatment on arrival.

In both the men's reception units, the attitude of staff towards inmates was direct and fair. However, the reality of the experience from a man's point of view was that after the journey to the Centre, he was placed with others in a holding room, referred to locally as 'the cage'. After waiting here he was called to change his clothes and have a shower. He received food and was placed in another holding room to eat it and await medical inspection and transfer to the wings. In at least one of these rooms a urinal was placed in full view in the corner. The adult unit was very scruffy, and the cages were particularly dirty with spilt food. The atmosphere was not tense. The reception clinic for men under 21 was similarly scruffy, but the atmosphere here was volatile. While we were there a fight broke out in the holding cell, and staff had to use force to remove two inmates from the rest. I remember the dim lighting and that this was the first time I was really shocked by what I saw.

It was apparent from our later conversations with prisoner groups that most inmates at Risley had been there before. In such circumstances it would not be difficult to overlook the impact of these reception procedures on those arriving at the Centre for the first time. On the night of our inspection, at the time when the fight broke out in the under-21 reception, a young man was standing, dressed only in a towel in front of an officer who was itemizing his clothing. When the noise of fighting broke out, the officer left to assist. The inmate stood alone, shivering with fear. Later he was placed in a cell on his own and left to await a hospital officer. It was his first time in prison and he faced a serious charge.

The medical examination of new arrivals at Risley was no more appropriate:

On the night of our inspection there were about twelve new inmates in the over-21 reception. They had to wait to see the doctor. He was due at 7pm. In fact he arrived at around 8.15 pm. Each new inmate was brought to see him separately. The first question he asked was 'Do you consider life worth living?' This was followed by a number of questions on physical health, and in some cases a brief chest examination, before a series of questions on the inmate's previous involvement with drugs, attempts on his own life, or other life-endangering activities. In each case, with the exception of the last, the response of inmates to the question of suicide was to dismiss it.

The last person to be seen was an inmate who had arrived at the prison with a police 'exceptional risk' form, which stated that he might have suicidal tendencies. On being asked the opening question, as to whether he considered life worth living, he answered 'No'. The doctor pressed him. Did he think he might take his own life? 'No,' replied the inmate. The doctor then, very firmly, asked him what he had meant when he said that life was not worth living. How could it not be worth living if he, the inmate, did not wish to take his own life? The inmate replied heatedly that he did not consider his own life was worth living because he had brought shame on his family, but this did not mean that he would, therefore, take his own life. The examination continued as before, and the inmate was marked as suitable for ordinary location.

I concluded:

The recent cleaning of the exteriors so as to remove the stains of excreta and other filth has made the building superficially less offensive, but B and C Wings and the conditions in the reception in particular are totally unacceptable. Such conditions would be bad enough in any penal establishment, but must be wholly condemned where the inmates are held on remand, unconvicted of an offence, and with the immediate stress of separation from family and approaching trial. Improvements could and should have been carried out before our inspection, but inadequacies of design appear to have laid the foundation of hopelessness and apathy.

A Young Offenders Institution, Lancaster Farms, was inspected in late 1994. The Preface of my report the following year said this:

There were many indications of a well-run, safe and constructive establishment. Lancaster Farms was very clean with no sign of any graffiti; cells were the tidiest and cleanest we have seen; evening association was more like a first-class, well-organized boys' club than a remand centre. Every adolescent had an opportunity to attend education, training or work which was relevant, and although there was the choice of staying in their cell doing nothing, not many chose to do so. One inmate told us, 'You are guaranteed to walk out with more than you walked in with.'

Through their clear and direct approach to the inmates, and their clear sets of rewards and sanctions, staff had established an orderly and controlled environment, that was equally open, fair and appreciated by those in their care. Volatile and unpredictable adolescents from deprived urban backgrounds were responding to the approach: to observe groups of youngsters smoking in a designated area in the association room, accepting the reason for that rule and respecting the furnishing of the rest of the room spoke volumes for what was being achieved.

Despite the high throughput of inmates the standard of care seemed to the Inspectorate to be an effective discharge of the duty of the Prison Service 'to help them lead law-abiding and useful lives in custody and after release'.

In the Conclusion of my report I wrote:

Lancaster Farms was within its first two years of operation and was well on the way to achieving its aim to be a model establishment for adolescents. The establishment was well designed and constructed, and had been maintained in good condition. The statement of purpose – 'our aim is to prevent the next victim' – typified the positive messages to inmates and staff which gave staff confidence in their ability and allowed them to develop initiatives.

The management team had learnt from the experiences of others in opening new establishments. There had been no serious disorder as there had been in some other establishments during their first two years of operation. Prison Service headquarters had perpetuated the error of allowing the number of inmates to rise too quickly after opening, but this had been dealt with successfully. Lancaster Farms provided a safe and controlled environment. There was a system of rewards and sanctions which gave a clear structure to young men with histories of non-conforming behaviour. Inmates knew what was expected of them and were confronted if their behaviour fell below acceptable standards.

The anti-bullying policy was central to good order. No inmates were separated from the rest of the population for their own protection. If bullying occurred, it was the bully who was separated and not the victim.

The management approach at Lancaster Farms was entirely positive:

Education, training and employment opportunities existed for all inmates. Most of the unconvicted responded to the encouragement to take part in something, though they could not be made to. There was a strong desire amongst staff to respond to suggestions for improvement.

The standard of care was high. We saw examples of good practice in catering, the probation service and health care.

We were particularly interested in the arrangements for the provision of the latter, which was based on contracts with a local general practice for primary and emergency care, with the local NHS Trust for in-patient care and with a psychiatrists to cover receptions and psychiatric in-patient care. Everyday management was carried out by a senior nurse. It could be a model for other establishments....

The central philosophy was that young men of this age group should be treated as adolescents, not as adults. All staff had taken part in a course developed in conjunction with the Trust for the Study of Adolescence entitled 'The Nature of Adolescence: Working with Young People in Custody'. We commend this training and we have recommended that all staff working with young people under 21 in the prison service should receive it.

Lancaster Farms is not unique as a good prison, run with education very much in mind. There are a number of HM prisons outside England with high standards. HM Prison Grand Cayman has devoted, though ill-paid, teachers, and a recidivist rate not exceeding 5 per cent. HM Prison St Helena is tiny, well kept and very successful.

These good prisons show what can be done. But it is not a very useful act to write about what will happen to prisons in the future. The outlook is gloomy, with policies encouraging overcrowding, and cutting of staff and budgets, so that many inadequate people will be deprived of the education and psychiatric help they need. The gloom extends: a dying remand prisoner is shackled, a woman prisoner in labour is shackled in what seems to be inhumanity on a shocking scale. In the long term the gloom may pass. I look forward to industrial prisons coupled with a far higher morale in the Prison Service.

It may be useful nevertheless to record what *should* happen in the future. Much of what should happen was set out in the Woolf Report and in the White Paper *Custody, Care and Justice: The Way Ahead for the Prison Service in England and Wales*, both published in 1991. My gloom does not extend to saying that it will not happen. In the Woolf Report there were twelve central recommendations many of which have not been achieved:

1. Closer co-operation between the different parts of the criminal justice system, including a national forum and local committees. This has largely been accomplished with the support of the judges.
2. More visible leadership of the Prison Service by a director-general who is seen to be the operational head and in day-to-day charge of the Service. Derek Lewis as Director-General was dramatically sacked in 1995 and, when he sued for unlawful dismissal, the taxpayer was obliged to pay him a very large sum in compensation. The Director-General, as is shown in the Chief Inspector's Report for 1996 is grossly overworked and inadequately supported.
3. Increased delegation of responsibility to governors. Governors are now to play a large part in deciding where the government's cuts are to fall.
4. An enhanced role for prison officers.
5. A compact or contract for each prisoner defining as far as possible his rights and duties in prison. This has not been attempted.

6. A national system of accredited standards with which, in time, each prison would be required to comply.

7. A new prison rule for control by the courts of numbers of prisoners, where the certified normal level of accommodation was exceeded. This recommendation was rejected by the government.

8. A timetable for sanitation for all prisoners by February 1996. This was largely met.

9. Better prospects for prisoners to maintain their links with families and the community through more visits and home leaves and through being located in community prisons as near to their homes as possible. In fact visits and home leaves have been greatly reduced and not improved, and with overcrowding nothing has been done to locate prisoners near their families. The importation of 'hulks' from America is not going to help to carry out this recommendation. These 'hulks', prison boats anchored near the towns in the rivers or the sea, were tried unsuccessfully as a means of holding prisoners in the eighteenth century, and there is no reason to think them likely to be more feasible now.

10. A division of prison establishments into smaller and more manageable and secure units. In fact prisons are becoming larger.

11. A separate statement of purpose, separate facilities and generally lower security categorization for remand prisoners.

12. An improved standard of justice within prisons, the giving of reasons to a prisoner for any decision which materially and adversely affects them.

The White Paper takes the Woolf Report a stage further. Kenneth Baker, the Home Secretary who commissioned the White Paper, called for prisons to be secure, stable, safe for prisoners and staff, just, caring and decent, productive and positive. It is interesting to note the recommendation by the government for positive prisons:

> The prisoner's time should be planned, in consultation with him or her, in a way which provides the opportunity where necessary for the individual to face up to what he or she has done and work towards ways of avoiding crime in the future; to increase social and physical skills and educational competence; and to make realistic preparations for release. Prisons should provide every opportunity practicable for prisoners to maintain links with home. Prisoners should be given opportunities for achieving something in prison which they can take forward following their release.

'The Government considers', says this remarkable White Paper,

that the priorities should be:

1. To improve necessary security measures.
2. To improve co-optation with other services and institutions, by working closely with the Probation Service and membership of a national forum and area committee.
3. To increase delegation of responsibility and accountability to all levels with clear leadership and a published annual statement of objectives.
4. To improve the qualities of jobs for staff.

5. To recognize the status and particular requirements of unconvicted prisoners.
6. To provide active and relative programmes for all prisoners including unconvicted prisoners.
7. To provide a code of standards for conditions and activities for prisons, which will be used to set improvement targets in the annual contracts made between prison governors and their area managers.
8. To improve relationships with prisoners, including a statement of facilities for each prisoner, sentence plans, consultations, reasons for decisions and access to an independent appeal body for grievances and disciplinary decisions.
9. To provide access to sanitation at all times for all prisoners.
10. To end overcrowding.
11. To divide the larger wings of prisons into smaller, more manageable units wherever possible.
12. To develop community prisons which will involve the gradual realignment of the prison estate into geographically coherent groups serving most prisoners within that area.

The White Paper was based not only on Woolf but on the Citizen's Charter of John Major, on the report of the House of Commons Education, Science and Arts Committee of 1990, on a report on Category A security by Messrs Gordon Lakes and Hadfield (both men with great knowledge and understanding of prisons) and on two reports for which I was responsible, one on suicide in prison which I have already mentioned, and one on an escape from Brixton prison. It firmly adheres to the prison 'Statement of Purpose', with its emphasis on security, humanity and helping prisoners to lead law-abiding lives. It provides what it claims, 'The Way Ahead'. 'This White Paper', it states, 'charts a course for the prison service in England and Wales for the rest of this century and beyond.'

But there are clearly gaps in the White Paper. The paper does not deal with the drug problem in prison. 'All prisoners', most sensibly writes the Chief Inspector General Sir David Ramsbotham in his 1995 annual report, 'come from a society where drugs are abundant, but sadly the drug culture that has been allowed to grow up in prisons, which includes bullying and debt, drags too many, including some who previously avoided the habit, into its clutches. At last there has been a recognition that a prison sentence presents society with an opportunity for tackling the problem with all sentenced prisoners that must be seized.'

Drugs create a problem which calls for a response in prison, from security, education and health. Mandatory drug testing (MDT) may well be helping: as yet there is no clear evidence. The sharper use of cameras in visit rooms and more frequent cell searching with dogs are the obvious advances by way of security. Drug testing must be followed by treatment and by full-scale programmes for addicted offenders, so that the time in prison can be used for discouraging addiction in the future, when the prisoner returns to the community.

Health care in prison is not very fully dealt with in the White Paper, partly because, in writing the Woolf Report, Lord Woolf and I did not see it as central to the problems which brought about the prison disturbances in 1990.

Obviously health was central to questions of suicide and self-harm, discussed in the Inspectorate report which was much used in preparing the White Paper.

The story of prisons is about swings of a pendulum, changes of heart. In the eighteenth century, Jeremy Bentham proposed prisons as an instrument to improve the character of the inmates. During the nineteenth century this idea began to fade. Early in the twentieth century there was a revival of optimism. The Gladstone Committee of that era had brought about a wider acknowledgement of the need for humanity. Training the young was established at Borstal. Alexander Paterson and others began to draw potential reformers of human nature into the Prison Service.

But, during the twenty years before I became involved in 1987, most observers were pessimistic. Prison reformers tended to believe that, except in rare cases, rehabilitation in prison was a failure and perhaps something of a mockery. Those in power, the establishment, the Home Office, saw prisons as necessary, possibly overfilled, and not capable of bearing too close an examination. Both groups had in common the belief that little good could emerge from any prison. The true purpose was, at vast expense, to contain dangerous men and women where, for the time being, they could not commit more crime. This is the concept behind the modern phrase 'Prison works'.

There was no dependable analysis of how prisons might be used in reducing crime. The reformers, after the lengthy onslaught on capital punishment by Margery Fry and her colleagues at the Howard League had been completed, were involved in improving standards and physical conditions. There was no resistance to this from the authorities save by way of a plea of lack of resources.

In the 1990s there came another swing. When the great disturbances at Strangeways in Manchester took place in 1990, Lord Woolf put forward the view that grievances of prisoners were at the heart of the problem and needed to be sympathetically examined. This view, though formally accepted, never really caught on with the establishment. Concern with prisons had moved to systems of financing, budgeting and management. Whether a market view of control and investment could be maintained, whether the setting up of an agency would help, whether prisons could be built and controlled by the private sector, how industrial warfare among staff could be reduced – all these became the focus of interest for both sides in the controversy.

This essay is based on a different approach. What are prisons for? Who are the inmates? What should we be doing to achieve a reduction in crime? Are we justified in writing off a sizeable proportion of our younger population as ineducable and suitable for permanent exclusion from the community? Elizabeth Fry had asked similar questions in an earlier century when she wrote: 'Punishment is not for revenge, but to lessen crime and reform the criminal.' It may be that she says it all.

Further Reading

Classics

Jeremy Bentham, *The Panopticon Writings* (Verso, 1995).

Michael Burn, *Mr Lyward's Answer: A Successful Experiment in Education* (Hamish Hamilton, 1956).

Jonathan Burnside and Nicola Baker, *Relational Justice: Repairing the Breach* (Waterside Press, 1994).

David Faulkner, *Darkness and Light: A Report for the Howard League* (Howard League, 1996).

Michel Foucault, *Discipline and Punish: The Birth of the Prison* (Penguin, 1974).

John Howard, *Prisons and Lazarettos* (Patterson Smith, New Jersey, 1973; reprint of 4th edn, 1792).

Michael Ignatieff, *A Just Measure of Pain* (Macmillan, 1971).

Mark Leech, *A Product of the System: My Life In and Out of Prison* (Gollancz, 1992).

Norval Morris and David J. Rothman, *Oxford History of Prisons: Practice of Punishment in Western Society* (Oxford University Press, 1995).

Leon Radzinowicz and Roger Hood, *The Emergence of Penal Policy in Victorian and Edwardian England* (Oxford University Press, 1990).

Tom Shannon and Christopher Morgan, *Invisible Crying Tree* (Doubleday, 1996).

Oscar Wilde, *The Soul of Man and Prison Writings* (Oxford
University Press, 1990).

Zeno, *Life* (Quality Book Club, 1968).

Useful Publications

Andrew Coyle, *The Prisons We Deserve* (HarperCollins,
1994).

Richard Creese, D. W. Bynum and J. Bearn (eds), *The Health of
Prisoners* (Rodopi, Amsterdam, 1995).

*Custody, Care and Justice: The Way Ahead for the Prison Service
in England and Wales* (HMSO, 1991).

Angela Devlin, *Criminal Classes: Offenders at School* (Waterside
Press, 1995).

Angela Devlin, *Prison Patter: A Dictionary of Prison Words and
Slang* (Waterside Press, 1996).

Roger Graef, *Living Dangerously: Young Offenders in Their Own
Words* (HarperCollins, 1992).

Katia Herbst and John Gunn, *The Mentally Disordered Offender*
(Mental Health Foundation, 1991).

Roy King and Kathleen McDermott, *The State of Our Prisons*
(Oxford University Press, 1995).

Mark Leech, *The Prisoners Handbook for 1995* (Oxford
University Press, 1995).

Derek Lewis, *Hidden Agendas: Politics, Law and Disorder*
(Hamish Hamilton, 1997).

Marian Liebmann, *Art Therapy with Offenders* (Jessica Kingsley,
1994).

Stephen Livingstone and Tim Owen, *Prison Law: Text and
Materials* (Oxford, 1993).

Roger Matthews and Peter Francis (eds), *Prisons 2000: An International Perspective on the Current State and Future of Imprisonment* (St Martin's Press, 1996).

Giles Radice (ed.), *What Needs to Change: New Visions for Britain* (HarperCollins, 1996).

Reports by HM Chief Inspector of Prisons for England and Wales (including *Annual Reports*), (Home Office, 1987–95).

Vivian Stern, *Bricks of Shame* (Penguin, 1987 and 1989).

Stephen Tumim, *The State of the Prisons* (The Goodman Lecture, 1994).

Stephen Tumim, *What Are Prisons For?* (Nicholas Bacon Memorial Lecture, 1991).

Lord Justice Woolf and Judge Stephen Tumim, *Prison Disturbances, April 1990* (HMSO, 1991).

PREDICTIONS

Asia and the Pacific
Climate
Cosmology
Crime and Punishment
Disease
Europe
Family
Genetic Manipulation
Great Powers
India
Liberty
Media
Men
Middle East
Mind
Moral Values
Population
Religion
Superhighways
Terrorism
Theatre
USA
Warfare
Women